Shattered No More

A child's journey from
trauma to triumph.

Trent Taylor & Pam Taylor

Trent Taylor
Pam Taylor

Printed in the United States of America

First Printing, 2015
ISBN - 13: 978-1515239987
ISBN - 10: 1515239985

Special Thanks

I would like to say "thank you" to everyone who has traveled this long and difficult journey by my side. Without your guidance, patience, support, and unconditional love, I would not be whom I am today. I can never find the words to express my gratitude to each and every one of you. You have helped me move beyond my past in order to help others.

My relationship with God has been the cornerstone in my healing process. While I faced many difficult times, I never lost faith in His plan for my life. God does not promise that we will not face adversity, but He does promise to walk by our side. I plan to remain open to God's will for my life and allow Him to use me for His good.

My Mom and Dad:

I cannot find the words to adequately express my feelings of gratitude and love toward you. You are the reason I was able to heal from my past. If God had not chosen you to be my parents, I would still be shattered. You taught me what it means to be a family. Because of your love, I have learned to trust and open my heart which was once closed. You never left me, never judged me and never gave up on me. You truly walked this journey along with me, held me when I cried and cheered me on as we broke through every painful memory. You have made me strong. I am able to share all of these details of my life because you instilled confidence and strength into a boy who once felt broken and incomplete. You will forever remain two of the most important people in my life. Thanks for pouring your entire beings into my healing and now giving me the opportunity to help others. I love you more than I ever imagined possible.

My Brother, Mike:

I am so sorry that you had to travel this painful journey, but I am so thankful that I had you by my side every step of the way. We have a bond that no one else will ever understand because we have been through so much. We are now strong, and I am so proud of who you are becoming. I look forward to a successful life with you as my best friend and brother.

Gram and Pop:

Thank you for being such an integral part of my life and my healing process from the day I arrived. You immediately opened your hearts and your home to me and have become two of the most important people in my life. You have fought for me and placed my needs ahead of your own on many occasions. I love you both more than you will ever understand.

Dan Kelly :

Thanks for inspiring me to write a book about my story. After reading your story, I gained the confidence and motivation to share mine. Thanks for guiding me through the process.

Special thanks to those who helped in completing this book process. Thank you for volunteering your time and talents to make this possible.

Doreen Arnott - Editing
Mary White - Editing
Mac Taylor - Editing
Jonna English - Cover Art
LeeAnn VanEyk - Photography
Jayce Williams - Photography

Dedication

This book is dedicated to all of the children in the foster care system and those who devote their lives to helping them heal. This book was written to remind you that you are not alone on this journey. Please remain hopeful and know that you can grow strong from each of your experiences along the way. Never lose hope.

Author's Notes

In order to protect anonymity, names in this book have been changed. This book was written from the perspective of a child with the intent to help others as they learn from the experiences of a young boy who traveled a journey from trauma to triumph. Since this book was written to inspire hope and not to harm, all identifying information has been changed to protect the privacy of those involved in the story.

Note To Families

This book was written to help those who have been through trauma as well as those who are supporting or raising children who have experienced trauma. While the majority of the book is age appropriate for all, the content is very emotional and may be difficult for some to read. We highly suggest reading the book prior to providing it to your child or reading it along with him/her. Various forms of abuse are discussed in a very general format but may be uncomfortable for younger readers. We also wanted to note that we are very aware that each child has a different story and experiences and will handle situations differently. We are, in no way, suggesting that individuals should follow the same path to healing that is depicted in this book. Every story is individualized, and as I further develop my abilities to mentor children, I will

assist each child along their own journey
regardless of how it compares to my story.

About the Authors

This mother and son team have experienced the healing journey together and have worked collaboratively to tell Trent's story through their first book, "*Shattered No More*". Pam and Trent often speak to large groups about their experiences and have plans for additional books, curriculum materials, and self-help guides in the future.

Trent is a *14*-year-old boy who has dedicated his life to helping children and families who have experienced trauma. At the young age of 14, Trent frequently speaks to large audiences about his experience in foster care. His compelling story has been featured in *The Wake Weekly, News and Observer*, and *919*

Magazine on multiple occasions. Trent has appeared on *WRAL News* and has starred in a promotional video. He also founded the Mercy for America's Children Kid's Division in 2012 and mentors many children in the process of being adopted through the foster care system. In addition, Trent serves on the Board of Directors for Mercy for America's Children as a Child Representative and has plans to increase his involvement within the organization as he grows older. Trent's efforts have been recognized by the community through recognition as a World of Children Award Nominee and a two-time Kohls Kids Award Nominee. This humble, young man reminds others frequently that everything he does is to bring awareness to the needs within the foster care system. Trent's willingness to openly share his story will inspire hope in the hearts of many.

Pam is an adoptive mother of two boys who have changed her life in unimaginable ways.

After a very complicated adoption process, Pam resigned from a 17-year career as a special education teacher to pursue her passion of forming a non-profit organization that promotes and supports adoption of children in the foster care system. In 2012, Pam and her husband, Mac, founded Mercy for America's Children. Pam serves as Executive Director for this thriving organization. She has an extensive background in Child Development and Behavior Analysis that has proven very valuable when supporting families who are fostering or adopting through the foster care system. Pam has successfully led this organization which is now very well known across the state of North Carolina. Pam has been recognized for her accomplishments and was named "Woman of the Year" by the National Association of Professional Women in 2014. In addition, she has been recognized by Who's Who Among American Business Women and was named a "Woman of

Influence " by the International Women's Leadership Association. Pam has a true heart for children and families and has dedicated her life to promoting positive change in her community.

In addition to founding Mercy for America's Children, Trent and Pam have created a Christian ministry called *Watch Me Rise*. To learn more about this ministry or to request a speaking engagement please visit www.watchmerise919.org.

Table of Contents:

Prologue

The primary goal when writing this book was to provide hope for both children and families who are struggling at various stages in the foster care system or adoption process. Translating my life into words was an extremely emotional process for both my mom and me. We anticipated the emotionality but did not fully realize the closure that this would provide. This process brought complete healing in many areas of my life.

In addition to providing hope, our desire was also to stir a movement of support for children in the foster care system. We are fully aware that not everyone is equipped to become a foster or adoptive parent, but support can be offered in many ways. Please visit the Mercy for America's Children website at www.mac-cares.org to learn more about our programs and services. Please consider taking action on behalf of the children in foster care. My sincere wish is for each of

them to have a journey that ends with a
forever family who loves them as much as my
family loves me.

-1-
Broken

My eyes scanned the large audience as I proudly walked to the stage to deliver my speech. Although I had practiced it over 20 times, I felt my heart pounding furiously as I mentally prepared to share my story with the 200 guests who were proudly adorned in their best tuxedos and formal dresses. It was more a feeling of excitement and anticipation than of fear. The large crowd was there to offer support to the organization started by my family nearly three years prior after they completed the adoption of my brother and me. As I took a moment to breathe, I felt consumed by the realization that I had finally been set free from a life of abuse, neglect and trauma and had been delivered to that moment. The realization was overwhelming. I was standing in front of a large group of influential adults, community leaders, and most importantly, family and friends whom I now called my own. I never imagined such a life, a life where I was no longer fearful and weak, a life where I now had a family that would love me unconditionally, a life where I was truly loved, a life where I could now make a difference in the lives of others. I choked back my emotion in order to enable myself to successfully deliver my life story at our 2nd Annual Charity Gala for Mercy for America's Children. In that moment, I openly exposed graphic details of my past while I delivered a message of hope for all of those who remained trapped in the foster care system. I smiled with true pride as I looked into the audience and saw teachers, mentors, and friends rise to their feet for a standing ovation. Upon the conclusion of my much anticipated speech, I felt somewhat vulnerable; I had just exposed my past to a large crowd. However, at the same time, I felt very empowered. I gained strength each and every time I was willing to open up about my past experiences.

As I exited the stage with a feeling of fulfillment, I was startled by a sudden, loud crashing sound toward the back left corner of the ballroom. A guest wearing a bold, red ball gown lost her grip on her shimmering water glass, and it hit the ground with a loud shatter. My heart fluttered as the familiar, but painful, sound evoked a very unpleasant memory. Each and every minuscule hair on my arms stood up as this sound immediately transported me to a painful moment from my past, a time when, just like the glass that hit the floor, my life was completely shattered.

Glass blew into a million tiny shards as I heaved my bicycle pump through my bedroom window with all my might in an angry rage. I was 4 years old, but I remember every vivid detail of that tragic moment. My little body was so full of emotions ranging from fear to pure anger, and I needed a way to release some of my pent up rage. After the glass exploded all over the bedroom floor, I realized that I had been injured as a result of my emotional tantrum. A few shards of glass had flown into my arm, and blood had begun to spill. In a strange way, I felt a sense of relief. The physical pain served as a brief distraction from the psychological and emotional pain that I endured on a daily basis. My window was shattered beyond repair, but so was my life, and no one seemed to care. The sad fact was that the adults who were supposed to be caring for me never noticed the shattered window or the bleeding lacerations on my arm. This came as no surprise because I often felt as if I did not even exist. I was invisible.

–2–

Baby Birds

I have always been amazed that, in nature, female animals are born with an innate desire and ability to protect and nurture their young. For example, a mother bird will tirelessly remain seated on her eggs and keep them safe and warm until it is time for them to crack out of their protective shell. After that miracle occurs, she will automatically do everything in her power to keep her little ones fed and safe until the day comes when they are ready to flap their tiny wings and fly into the world on their own. She puts her own needs aside and spends her days searching for worms to feed her babies. I have even witnessed a mother bird fight to the death to defend her babies. Since this is a primal instinct in the animal kingdom, one would naturally assume that humans would also possess this same instinct to care for their young. Unfortunately, I can attest to the fact that this is not always the case.

Through no fault of my own, I was born into a family of extreme dysfunction. A therapist once explained to me that this was just bad luck. Both my maternal and paternal birth family were filled with a tangled and extensive history of abuse, neglect, mental illness, incest, and on the maternal side, some abnormal behaviors that are often exhibited by religious cults. From an early age, I felt trapped and feared that I would never break free from the impenetrable chains of abuse. Fortunately, God had other plans for my life. I would first need to endure a five year journey that would be the most painful years of my life. To this day, when I look at a nest, I am often envious of the baby birds. They are loved and protected by their mother, so why was I not protected?

I was born on December 30, 2000 at 10:47 a.m. I was born with APGAR scores in the normal range through a very typical birth process. What was not normal was that I entered the world into a family that was filled with extreme dysfunction. Most babies enter the world greeted by parents who have been eagerly anticipating their arrival. Many parents dream of the day their baby will enter the world so that they can begin life as a family unit. At the time of my birth, my older brother (age 4) and sister (age 2) were already experiencing various forms of abuse and neglect. I entered a world of chaos and unrest and learned from infancy that my basic needs would not be met by those around me. According to my records, I was known as "the swing baby." I was simply placed in a swing for many hours at a time and left to cry on my own so that my birth mother would not be required to attend to my basic needs. I was invisible to the people who were supposed to love me the most.

Now that I am older and have studied child development and psychology at length, I am aware of how much damage can be inflicted during this period of development. When I look at images of a mother and child, I often see visions of nurture and love with the mother lovingly holding her baby close to her heart. This appears strange and unfamiliar to me. I do not have one single memory of being held or nurtured by my birth mother, not one single solitary memory of being soothed, touched, or loved in any way. I spent nearly five years in the home with my birth family. During this vital period of development, I experienced domestic violence, extreme neglect, and other forms of abuse that still haunt me to this day. My earliest memories of this environment still evoke feelings of anger, sadness, disappointment, abandonment, and feelings of unworthiness.

The years spent with those who gave birth to me were lived out in a small, white, single-wide trailer in rural North Carolina. This home was in such disrepair that it should have been condemned. The trailer had three bedrooms as well as a living room and a kitchen that was rarely utilized. I grew up surrounded by such clutter and filth that I would not wish it on my worst enemy. We did not own any cleaning supplies such as a vacuum or broom. As a result, food wrappers, crumbs, banana peels, and other trash would simply pile up in various locations of the house. Being surrounded by filth became our norm. I once watched a large, squirming cockroach eating a rotten banana peel that was located behind the couch. No one bothered to pick it up. It remained there until it slowly rotted away through the disintegration process. Many other food items and trash would simply be tossed to the nasty floor. Needless to say, my siblings and I left this horrific environment any time we got a chance. Although we were young, ranging in age from three to seven, and should not have been out of the house by ourselves, we frequently wandered off into the neighborhood in an attempt to escape the chaos and seek some normalcy.

My birth father, Cameron, was rarely home. He spent his days driving a recycling truck under the assumption that our birth mother was monitoring my siblings and me. He worked very long hours and came home utterly exhausted. When he was present, a significant amount of yelling, cursing, and domestic violence ensued toward our birth mother. I once watched him push my birth mother into a countertop with all of his might after a very lengthy, one-way screaming match.

My birth mother, Blair, was at home most days but spent long periods of time isolated in her bedroom. She spent countless hours on the internet. If she was not connecting with strange men through online chat rooms, she was sleeping. She slept for very lengthy periods of time. We felt as if we were living on our own. As a result, Travis, Samantha, and I, were forced to develop ways to meet our own primal needs.

To this day, I find describing my birth mother extremely difficult. The best description I can find is "empty shell." I do not recall her ever showing any emotion toward me; I have no memory of either positive or negative emotion, only emptiness. I have never met another person who was capable of living life without expressing emotion like my birth mother.

Maslow, a famous psychologist, talks about a hierarchy of needs. At the bottom of his detailed pyramid are physiological needs. Until these needs are met, humans are unable to move to other areas of growth and development. Food is a basic physiological need, but it is also a manner in which children are nurtured and loved. In our society, families gather together around the dinner table socially, as a collective unit, to discuss the day, share moments together and enjoy a great meal. Although many families do not have the opportunity to do this daily, most are able to do this on occasion.

In the five year span that I spent with my birth family, I can recall only one meal that Blair cooked for our family. I vividly recall her opening a bag of frozen peas and heating them in a pot on the stove. During that moment, I had a vague glimmer of hope that she was changing her ways and would begin to care for us. I clung to that hope and savored those peas simply because she had taken the time to warm them for us. Unfortunately, that was the only meal (if you consider peas a meal) that she ever provided for us. Because I was in a neglectful situation, I grasped on to the smallest act and hoped and prayed that I mattered enough for someone to acknowledge me. However, the acknowledgement never came. In my mind, I was not worthy of her time.

I was forced to meet the basic survival need of eating on my own. Having my stomach ache from sheer emptiness became an unforgettable feeling. I often fell asleep with hunger pangs. The feelings of true hunger will never be erased from my mind. The utter emptiness in my stomach felt as if my body was eating itself from the inside out. My older brother and sister were often spotted wandering the local street in search of food. As a sibling group, we developed a hunting and gathering technique; we searched for food within our own home as well as the surrounding streets. I once discovered a bottle of Log Cabin syrup located in a high cabinet above the stove. On a mission for anything to fill my chronically empty stomach, I propelled myself onto the decaying stovetop to reach into the cabinet. I stealthily drank syrup from the bottle in fear of getting caught. The sickeningly sweet syrup was the best thing I had ever tasted. Looking back, the likelihood of getting caught was minimal since we were typically left unattended to raise ourselves. I think I would have felt some comfort in getting caught in the act because at least I would have known that someone cared enough to be aware of my dangerous actions.

In 2002, my younger brother, Brian, was born and brought into the same chaotic and unsafe environment as the rest of us. Immediately, we knew that his basic needs would not be met unless we stepped up to care for him. Our mother's lack of attention demanded that we take care of another tiny human being who was completely incapable of tending to his own needs. My older sister, Samantha, taught herself to prepare bottles for him and attempted to change his diapers. She had often completed these tasks with her tattered baby doll, but it proved to be a lot more challenging on a live human being who would cry and squirm. She was a five-year-old child who was forced into parenting an infant. She filled the role of mother for this crying, screaming child while the woman who gave birth to him was physically present in the home but confined herself to her bedroom and acted as if she were living alone.

As time passed, I also suffered physical abuse and violence at the hand of an additional relative. In addition to Travis and Brian, I had an older half brother named Allen. Truthfully, I never really understood where he came from or how he fit into this dysfunctional group of people who were supposed to be my family. He periodically walked through the door and stayed for long periods of time. He was a teenager who was dealing with raging hormones and very unpredictable mood swings. I saw the anger and hurt in his brown eyes as they glared at me across the room. He lashed out in unprovoked moments of anger and rage by throwing matchbox cars, breaking doors, and punching holes in the walls. I did not understand this at the time, but he was filled with rage and anger because he was suffering extreme abuse that would come to light much later. His story was not so different from mine.

As if extreme neglect and domestic violence were not enough, I was experiencing other unspeakable forms of abuse that I kept secret for many years to come. I was hiding some very deep secrets that were destroying me from the inside out, abuse that was so painful that I was determined to take it to the grave with me. It was the ultimate form of betrayal. I had no safe people in my life, no one to tell about this pain that was destroying me. I woke up each morning in utter fear: fear of starving, fear of being hurt, fear of never being loved, fear of remaining invisible forever. Feelings of unworthiness would flood my mind like a tsunami. No words exist to describe what happened to my mind when those who gave birth to me did not find me worthy of basic care and love. I remember feelings of complete hopelessness and despair. I have heard descriptions of people who consumed 10 cups of highly caffeinated coffee, and I lived every day with similar feelings. My adrenaline was constantly rushing and wearing down my weak body. I remained in fight or flight mode at all times. I had to stay very vigilant and aware of my surroundings to ensure my safety. This was no way for a young boy to spend his childhood. However, this was how I spent mine.

–3–

Foster Care - Here We Come

Next to our dilapidated trailer was a small, green house in which a tiny, gray-haired woman lived. As far as I could tell, she lived alone. She consistently demonstrated a very welcoming smile and wore small black glasses that hung low on her face. I often saw her outside, playing fetch with her hyperactive Jack Russell Terrier. Although she was very quiet, she seemed to be glancing our way as we wandered down the street unattended in our frequent search for food. We often caught her peering our direction and saw the concerned look on her face as her smile dropped. In the back of my mind, I secretly imagined her learning about our situation and helping us escape from our prison-like life of neglect and abuse. I found out later, when reading court documents, that she had been considering contacting authorities for a number of months. However, she had been issued verbal threats from my maternal grandmother, Lillith. Since the Department of Social Services became involved in our lives shortly after her apparent interest, I guessed that this quiet neighbor must have mustered up the courage to make the much-needed report. Social workers began coming and going from our home on what seemed like a daily basis. I added them to the list of people that I felt certain could not be trusted. I overheard these workers issue multiple requests to have the house cleaned up. This did not sound like an overwhelming task, only a suggestion to clean enough to have the environment declared safe. Each time my birth parents agreed, but they never complied with the simple requests. Instead, they continued with their selfish and damaging ways. Since they were clearly not parenting safely and effectively, the workers from the Department of Social Services also asked them to attend some parenting classes and therapy sessions. While part of me hoped that they would change, I knew in the depths of my soul that this would never come to pass. Despite the threats of losing their children, my birth family continued their egocentric and self-serving ways and did not comply with the very minimal requirements set forth by Social Services.

I attended a local day care and enjoyed this escape from the daily hellacious chaos that had become my life. At least in this setting, I had people who were financially rewarded for attending to my basic needs. They were strangers, but at least they acknowledged my existence and provided me with a safe environment in which I could escape my thoughts and fears.

One afternoon, instead of riding the bus home from daycare, my paternal grandfather, Mason, arrived to pick us up. My paternal grandparents had minimal presence in my life prior to this moment. I was familiar with them but had not developed a close and connected relationship. He explained to my brothers and me that we would be staying at his house for a little while. At the time, I had no idea that I had just entered the U.S. Foster Care System through what is called a kinship placement and would never return to my birth parents again. I was flooded with confusion and a very strange mix of emotions. Stories are commonly told of children who were devastated when leaving their birth parents, but mine was different. I was so invisible and neglected that I never had the opportunity to bond in the way that a child is intended to bond with his or her parents. While I felt emotional pain from the neglect and abuse, I never grieved being removed from my birth parents. Some therapists and mental health professionals would argue that this is not possible, but I was relieved to be moving to a new home. I felt hopeful that I would be acknowledged and fed at the very least.

Although little trauma was associated with me being removed from my birth parents, I was deeply pained when I learned that my sister, who had been serving as a caretaker for Brian and me, was being taken away from us. Samantha was the only nurturing force in my life and did her best to serve in the parental role even though she was only two years older than me. She was being separated from us for reasons that were unknown to me at the time. While my conflicting emotions were flooding my thoughts, I managed to choke back the tears and focus on our basic needs and safety. With Samantha gone, the job of protecting my brother became mine. I had to be strong.

The yellow house where my grandparents lived was warm, welcoming, and very clean compared to my previous home. It even smelled clean. As I looked around, I felt that this was a home where I would be fed and kept safe. I remember opening the refrigerator and being delighted by the sight of eggs, milk, fruit, and other food. Actual blankets were lying on the bed, and the trash was in the trash can where it belonged. My paternal grandmother, Diana, was a kind, christian woman who ran a home day care. Because of her child-centered career, there were many toys and games made available for our enjoyment. I spent countless hours playing with the superhero action figures. This became a favorite pastime because I was able to pretend that I was somewhere else; it allowed me to possess amazing powers to escape my crazy world.

Mason and Diana introduced us to church and the concept of God for the first time. We looked forward to attending church each week where we watched Mason strum his bass guitar in the praise band. Since I was at a point in my life where I was searching for any sense of peace, I immediately clung to the hope I found in God and his message of unconditional love. Despite my difficult circumstances, I began to pray and develop a personal relationship with Him. While at times I certainly questioned how a good and loving God could allow me to endure such pain, I remained faithful to Him and trusted in his plan for my life. I clung to the hope I found in God.

I slowly lowered my guard as I felt somewhat safe in this new environment. While I was protected from contact with my birth parents and provided with food each and every day, I soon realized that this environment was not completely safe after all. In this home, I was expected to share a room with my older brother, Travis. In addition, I was often expected to share a bed with him. While Mason and Diana meant well, I was placed in harm's way, and I continued to quietly suffer abuse at the hands of Travis. He was my older brother who should have protected me and kept me safe, but he had become one of my primary abusers. I was housing so many painful secrets in my young mind; every day was spent consumed by confusion and fear. This home that was deemed safe by Social Services was the polar opposite. Those around me, both adults and children, continued to hurt me in unimaginable ways.

Some people may wonder why I did not reveal all the hurt that I was suffering. Just like most children, I had an innate desire to respect and trust those who were older. I wanted to believe that brothers, parents, and other relatives would never cause me harm. Grasping the reality of the situation was too painful for my already hurting heart. I was verbally threatened on a daily basis. I was fearful that if I exposed the abuse, my life would spiral further down this path of destruction.

A few months passed and I endured my silent hell each and every day. Because of the continued abuse and suppressed emotions, I exhibited some significant behavior issues in this setting. I was filled with fear, uncertainty and a growing rage that would often manifest through my behaviors. I was later informed that my behaviors became too much for our grandparents to handle. As a result, we were ripped away and placed in the home of complete and total strangers. We were officially headed to foster care.

–4–

Pop Tarts and Hot Pockets

I was told to gather my few belongings and place them into a very old and tattered duffel bag that smelled of mothballs. A woman who was a complete stranger and wore a badge to identify herself arrived at the home of my grandparents. She explained to us in a very terse manner that we would be moving. I immediately felt like I wanted to vomit as the fear of the unknown consumed me. I was anticipating a new home, new school, and new friends. All adults in my life had proven that they could not be trusted, even those who felt they were keeping me safe. These fears were debilitating. Fear, sadness, and anger were contributing to a large, protective mechanism that was already forming in my impressionable mind. I was convinced that I needed to protect myself by not allowing people to love me . I was determined to build a wall to protect my heart and mind.

When I heard that we were relocating, I hoped and prayed that Travis would be placed in a different home so that I could be spared of the abuse that continued in secret. I remained hopeful that someone had discovered what he had been doing to me. However, my hopes were shattered when I learned that he was being placed in the same home as my younger brother and me. Those shattered hopes became a total nightmare when I learned that he would be sharing a room with us again. With all these fears and nightmares, Brian and I entered the home of Mr. and Mrs. Thomas.

I soon learned that Mr. Thomas was a state trooper. He was a large caucasian man with a tight, military-style haircut. He carried himself with a sense of confidence and pride. My behavior immediately corrected due to fear of consequences that could be issued by this intimidating man. I noticed that Mr. Thomas struck fear in the heart of my older brother and became hopeful that this fear would stop him from perpetrating on Brian and me. I prayed frequently and was cautiously hopeful. My prayers were answered and my older brother never touched me while in the Thomas home.

Mr. and Mrs. Thomas treated us well. They fed us on a regular basis. On rare occasions, they would prepare a home-cooked meal, but most meals consisted of Hot Pockets or Pop Tarts. I consumed so many Hot Pockets and Pop Tarts that, to this day, I cannot even stand to watch the TV commercials for those horrid foods.

This family took the time to teach us some basic life skills that had been previously overlooked. Although I was 6 years old, I had never been taught basic hygiene. They taught Brian and me how to brush our teeth, take a shower, change our clothing and tie our shoes. This provided me with a new-found sense of independence. For the first time, I was able to successfully meet a few of my own basic needs.

While this was by far the best environment I had experienced in my early years, things still happened that damaged my emotional well-being and contributed to the distrust of those around me. Mr. and Mrs. Thomas had a 16-year-old biological daughter who slept in the room next to our room. She often babysat us when her parents were not at home. Megan was a fiery redhead who had the stereotypical attitude and temper to match. Her actions frequently made it clear that she did not enjoy sharing her home or her parents with Brian and me. When the adults were out of the home, she frequently punished me by making me sit on a very high railing. This railing was on the second story of the home and overlooked the living room, creating a 20 foot drop from railing to floor. She often forced me to sit on this railing. As I sat in utter terror, I cried and pleaded with her to let me down. My heart pounded and I gasped for breath as I sat in utter fear. I knew that if I fell, I would be severely injured and possibly plummet to my death. She also delivered the same punishment to my younger brother when she was annoyed by his behavior. One evening, Brian was pushed over the railing and plummeted to the first floor. Although he miraculously landed on a couch below, I felt certain that he was going to die. He developed a large, black and purple mark on his back. For purposes of self preservation, Megan attempted to nurse Brian back to health while threatening to deliver the same fate to me if I told anyone what had really happened.

I again learned that I could not trust the people who were supposed to take care of me. No place was safe. I could not help but hope that another move was on the horizon. I was beginning to sense a pattern of constant movement from home to home. Before too much time had passed, the social worker

came and told us that we were moving again.
This had become a common pattern for me.
As I packed my few meager items, I mentally
prepared myself for the unknown yet again.

–5–

Cigarettes and Pit Bulls

I breathed a huge sigh of relief when I learned that my next placement would be with some familiar faces. My maternal uncle and his wife had agreed to take us into their home. When I entered the small home that would become my new residence, I immediately choked on the familiar smell of stale cigarette smoke. My birth father was a chain smoker, so I knew that unpleasant scent all too well. An older woman lived in the home who reeked of cigarettes. The horrible smell had penetrated her clothing and even her wrinkly skin. I later learned that she was the mother of my Aunt Jessica. To this day, I cannot tolerate the smell of cigarettes. I am truly amazed at how powerful the sense of smell can be. Certain smells bring back very vivid memories for me. Cigarette smell evokes bad memories. Being exposed to that smell transports me back to many unpleasant memories from my past.

As we entered the home, we were greeted by an extremely tall pit bull who appeared very threatening. Muscles rippled on this dog who approached us with a leaping bark. This was not how I had hoped to be greeted in my new home. My mind flooded with all of the worries of the unknown and questions about the future: "Would we be fed? Would we be safe? Where would I sleep? Where would I attend school?" In spite of the terrifying greeting, I was hopeful that this might become a more permanent placement. I wanted this turmoil to end. Instead, this became another stop on my lengthy journey.

Many people in my life, including social workers, therapists, and others, frequently made the assumption that I had a longing desire to return to my birth parents. While I strongly desired the permanency of a family, I had no desire to return to my birth family who had let me down so many times in the past. Truthfully, I did not even know what the word "family" truly meant.

While this home was also filled with chaos, it felt safer. My biological uncle, Jonathan, was a police officer. This brought a sense of security for me since I had the false assumption that all police officers held high moral standards and were generally people of upstanding character. While that is the case the majority of the time, I now know that a badge does not ensure morality. My aunt, Jessica, was very kind and nurturing. She cooked us meals which was a much welcomed change.

A child by the name of Alexander came to visit on occasion. He was Jonathan's son from a previous relationship. My older brother, Travis, continued his abusive ways and acted out toward several others children, including Alexander and Brian. During this time, he also continued his regular abuse towards me in secret. I kept the secrets bottled inside of me out of fear. However, I felt that his actions would soon be exposed because he was acting out toward other children as well as me. I hoped and prayed that someone would discover his actions and rescue me from this excruciating pain.

My secret wish was granted when, shortly after we arrived at my aunt and uncle's house, my uncle discovered that Travis had acted inapropriately toward Alexander. Jonathan reacted in anger and punished all involved, including those who had no ability to defend themselves. No help was offered in the form of therapy or other services, just punishment. I knew this meant that we would be leaving again. Knowing it was only a matter of time, I simply waited for the contact from my social worker.

During my time in foster care, I became skilled in the art of reading people well in order to protect myself from physical and emotional harm to the best of my ability. I approached all new relationships with extreme caution. Over the tears I had many social workers come and go from my life. During this phase of my journey, I met our new social worker named Deborah. As she introduced herself, I sensed that she was different from most of the other adults in my life. She was immediately warm and served as a source of comfort in my world filled with unrest. Unlike others who had come and gone, she gave me evidence, from the moment we met, that she truly cared about our well-being. While her position as a social worker evoked a healthy fear, I also felt certain that she was going to change my life in a significant way. I did not know it at the time, but Deborah would remain by our side for the remainder of our painful journey through the foster care system.

During this period of my life, the court ordered supervised visitations with our birth parents. The judge and social workers clung to the hope that my birth family would comply with their suggestions in order to reunify our family. We were scheduled to visit with our birth parents one time per month. My anger brewed each time we traveled in the car to the local D.S.S. office where we would spend one hour attempting to spend quality time with our birth parents while being observed through a 2-way mirror. When we arrived, we were never greeted with hugs or loving words of being missed at home as one might expect.

During each visit, I entered a room where my birth mother would simply remain seated in the corner with her empty and blank expression. I rarely, if ever, attempted to engage her in any form of contact. Based on past experience, I knew my attempts would be wasted and rejection was eminent. Even when prompted by social workers to greet her children, she remained silent and stone-faced. Instead, I always chose to focus my energies on my birth father who at least acknowledged my existence in the room. When laying eyes on him, I became so filled with hatred that I was unable to control my actions. I made a habit of launching myself onto him from behind and punching him in the back while screaming with all my might. The social workers allowed this to happen in order to see how my birth parents would respond. I was not shocked that my birth mother remained glued to her isolated seat in the corner, while my birth father attempted to peel me from his body. However, I was baffled that my birth parents truly had no understanding of the reasons for my anger. Because this man and woman who gave birth to me had not taken care of me, I had been on a whirlwind, torturous journey since birth. Their inability to understand the anger their actions had caused magnified my pain.

Our visitation at the local Department of Social Services continued over the next few months. The court ordered that my birth parents were not to have contact with us unless supervised by my social worker. My uncle had two reasons to obey the court order. First, he was a police officer. Second, he was a blood relative who was awarded with the task of keeping us safe. However, just like the other adults in our life, he also failed us. He eventually allowed our birth parents to have access to us in his home. Since he allowed my birth parents to have unsupervised visitation, the Department of Social Services deemed this placement unsafe.

One day at school, I was engaged in my regular art class with hands full of clay when a message over the loudspeaker called me to the office. Like any typical child getting summoned to the principal's office, I became anxious about what was to follow. I felt my heart rate increase as I neared the front office.

When I reached the office, I saw the familiar face of my social worker, Deborah. I immediately knew that she was there to tell me about another change. Although I loved her very much, I knew that she was the one who would deliver the news to me about my life. She explained that we would be moving again. As she shared more information with me, I thought I heard the words, "Your older brother, Travis, will be going to a different home." Those words triggered the question in my mind, "Could it be that they uncovered the secrets that I had kept locked in my head for so long?" While nearly every part of me dreaded the unknown of moving again, I grasped to the glimmer of hope that I would be protected from the actions of my older brother. I learned that I would be moving into the home of complete strangers yet again. The repeated failures of my extended birth family members had made it clear that they were either unable or unwilling to meet our needs. The total rejection caused many doubts and questions to flood my mind, "How many times will the people in my life fail me? Why was no one willing to take care of me and love me?" I learned to shut off my emotions so that they would not hurt so much. I constructed my protective wall high and strong; I believed that I could never trust anyone again. I truly believed that if I refused to let people into my heart, then it could not get broken again.

As I once again packed my few belongings into my worn-out bag to get ready for another move, I stifled my emotions. Each time I moved to a new home, I was forced to leave behind most of my toys, clothes, and a piece of myself. Each move was chipping away at my ability to trust people. My brother and I placed our items in the car and said our goodbyes to our aunt and uncle as we were headed out into the unknown again. The car rumbled as we headed to our meeting point where we would be delivered to our next caregivers.

We arrived at a local McDonald's where our social worker bought us chocolate-dipped ice cream cones to lessen the sting of being forced to relocate again. While wiping dripping ice cream from my mouth, I caught a glimpse of an older woman covered in wrinkles. She wore glasses and peered at us through them as she bent her head toward the floor. She appeared tired and somewhat irritated. We had obviously interrupted her plans for the evening. Our social worker made the awkward introductions, and off we went to yet another "home."

I asked myself every day if this had become my life. I felt homeless with nothing but the few items in my little bag. I had lost every piece of myself. Little did I know that my prayers would soon be answered and this would be my final stop before God began turning my life around. While I experienced tremendous loss on every step of this painful journey, I never forgot the God that had been by my side the entire time. My relationship with Him grew during each and every painful step.

-6-

Horseradish

As my brother and I traveled to our new destination, the old familiar rush of adrenaline flowed through every muscle in my body. I clenched my teeth so hard that my jaw began to hurt. The thought that no adults in the world could be trusted was firmly planted in my mind. The only sense of relief associated with this move was that my older brother, Travis, would no longer be placed in the home with us. While I knew that I would no longer be subjected to that horrific abuse, the basic fears remained. Another positive factor was that our sister was located in a foster home located nearby, so we would be able to see her on a more regular basis.

After a 20-minute drive that seemed like an eternity, Brian and I arrived at a rather small house with a large inviting yard. We were excited about the idea of running and playing outside as a form of escape. For the first time, we were each given our own room. While this may sound exciting, I was very afraid. The room was filled with dolls that sent shivers down my spine. They reminded me of dolls that I had seen in horror movies at an inappropriately young age. I went to bed at night in total fear and buried myself so deeply in the covers that I could not breathe and woke up in a panic, covered in sweat.

While her intentions seemed good when we arrived, our foster parent began to prove otherwise. Her punishment methods were cruel and unethical. Her favorite punishment was to force-feed us horseradish by the spoonful. I remember swallowing this horrible mixture and feeling like I wanted to projectile vomit. I reported this to our social worker during our monthly visit. When confronted, our foster parent emphatically denied that she had ever used this form of cruel punishment. In addition to the horseradish punishment, she also made some horrible comments that changed the way I thought about myself and my changing body. I later realized that the comments were very damaging to my self esteem. Once again, I was in a place where the adults who were supposed to be caring for me were causing further damage through cruel punishments, damaging comments, and blatant lies to other adults. My wall was officially built. It was like Fort Knox, and I was determined that it would never come down. I absolutely refused to let adults or others into my heart; I could not allow them because I knew that it would end in unspeakable pain. During my time in this home, I learned that the judge had finally decided that my birth family was not going to comply with the minimal requirements set forth to reunify our family. The Department of Social Services, the Guardian Ad Litem (State appointed child advocate), and the court system decided that nearly four years had been long enough and the process of terminating parental rights should begin.

Our therapist began introducing the concept of adoption in our weekly therapy sessions. While I had no concept of what the term "adoption" meant, I began to understand that could bring change for my future. This concept provided hope that I would find a way out of this continuous cycle of destruction that had been slowly and systematically destroying me. Although it was difficult, I clung to my relationship with God and never lost faith in His plan for me. God was my only hope. I began to trust that I had endured all of this pain and turmoil for a purpose; I just did not know what that purpose was yet. I did not know it yet, but my life was about to change forever. As we packed our bag for a fun day of water skiing on a local lake, I felt a sense of hope that I had never felt before. I knew that my life was about to change, but how?

_7_

Get Off the Dock

I shoved my swimsuit that hardly fit me
any longer into my blue cinch sack and waited
anxiously for my social worker to pick up
Brian and me to drive us to the outdoor event
at Lake Christy. This private, man-made lake
located near Greenville, North Carolina was
owned by the Overton family. This family was
well-known in the Raleigh area for owning
several boating shops. Christy Overton had
started a mission a number of years ago to
help connect children who were awaiting
adoption with families who were seeking an
adoptive placement. "A Day To Remember"
was an annual event where children awaiting
adoption enjoyed a day of fun on the lake,
including boating, skiing, swimming, and
other water games. In addition, families who

were licensed and waiting to adopt came out to meet the waiting children face-to-face.

While Brian and I waited for Deborah to arrive, I felt a sense of excitement and happiness even though I had no idea what was ahead. I was excited to have a day away from the constraints of my foster home. I was also anxious to see my sister, Samantha, whom I had not seen for several months. Mrs. Deborah finally pulled into the gravel driveway, and we jumped in the car and started on our journey to what would prove to be the critical turning point in my life. On the way I received the obligatory lecture from my Mrs. Deborah to be on my best behavior, and, as always, I agreed. I had learned that if I told adults exactly what they wanted to hear, things were made easier for me. After nearly 90 minutes in the car, we pulled down the long tree-lined driveway that eventually ended at a beautiful, crystal-clear lake with a large wooden dock. A crowd of people were gathered on the dock, and I saw mounds of chicken sandwiches and other treats. If for no other reason than an unlimited amount of food, I knew that this was going to be a good day. Our social worker placed a blue band on our wrists. Although I was somewhat curious as to the purpose of this band, I never inquired because I was too eager to get started and enjoy the inviting water. As time passed, I noticed more and more adults had arrived and were given red bands. Many of the adults appeared nervous as they scanned the children in attendance. I overheard some of the older boys explaining that the blue bands were for children who were awaiting adoption while the red bands were for families hoping to adopt children. Although I was only eight years old, I had gathered enough information to realize that we were attending what was called a match event. I overheard a group of teens saying that they had attended over 16 match events, and no one was ever interested in adopting them. After hearing this information, I chose to put up my superficial wall and protect myself from the thought that I could possibly find an adoptive family. If it had not happened for the teens around me, it most certainly would not happen for my younger brother and me. Instead of dealing with my heavy emotions, I decided to plunge into the fun and get what I could out of this time on the lake.

After a short time passed, a very large, muscular man with a military-type haircut began playing with Brian and me in the refreshing lake water. This man poured every ounce of his attention on us. He played with us for hours and made us laugh and smile for the first time in years. He picked us up and threw us into the water, creating a giant splash every single time. We were having so much fun that all the other kids seemed to gather around to join the fun. While he played with other children, he continued to focus his attention on our needs. Receiving so much direct attention was strange and somewhat uncomfortable for me. I wanted to enjoy the moment and soak in every second of love that he was willing to share but I could feel myself putting up my wall. Past experience had taught me that this fun was going to cease in only a few short hours and that I would never see him again. He taught us new skills, encouraged us to be brave, and laughed with us the entire day. I caught myself daydreaming about having a family who would share moments like this. I caught a glimpse of his red wristband and recalled what the older boys had said. That red band meant that this amazing man was there to meet children that he could potentially add to his family through adoption. Questions of doubt flooded my mind: "Why was he focussed on Brian and I? With all of the other amazing children around us, why did he stay by our side the entire day? "

A whistle sounded and indicated the start of the next event on the schedule which was lunch on the dock followed by a brief program. This kind and gentle giant of a man who had been showering us with attention introduced himself as Mr. Mac. He took us by the hand and led us to the dock to meet his wife. When I first glanced at her, she looked like an angel. She was helping my sister comb her hair after her time in the water. She spent nearly 30 minutes nurturing my sister who was so desperately craving attention and love. I later learned that she was very ill that day with strep throat and was unable to get in the water. Despite not feeling well, she had a warm and welcoming smile, and I sensed that she wanted to wrap her warm and loving arms around us from the minute we met.

We sat together and enjoyed an absurd amount of food, including unlimited Mountain Dew. As a group, we listened to a story about how we must "Get off the Dock" and step out on faith in this life if we expected to succeed. As we sat and listened to the presentation, I could not help but fantasize about being a family. These two amazing people had already shown us more kindness, love, and attention in six short hours than I had received over the span of my lifetime. I soon realized that my sister was also toying with the same fantasy as she began to ask Mrs. Pam when she could come and live with them. She repeatedly stated that she wanted them to become her mom and dad. Mrs. Pam was obviously overcome with emotion as she wiped the tears from her eyes and explained that they must follow the guidelines set forth by the Department of Social Services. We spent the last hour together playing frisbee, running, playing, and simply soaking every ounce of affection offered by these two wonderful people. As the day came to a close, I remember the overwhelming sadness that attacked as I was hit with the reality that I may never see them again. I had finally met two people who seemed to truly love me, and they were leaving me. Just like everyone else, they were leaving. I watched their car pull away and wiped a tears from my emotionally exhausted eyes. I felt like I was watching my dream fade away.

On the drive home, I repeatedly asked Mrs. Deborah if we could go live with Mr. Mac and Mrs. Pam. She was very evasive and explained that we would have to wait and see. This amazing day had come and gone, and I was headed back to my foster home where I felt like nothing. As I was falling asleep that night after a physically and emotionally exhausting day, I tightly gripped the dog tag necklace that I was given at the "Day To Remember" event earlier that day. It was a dog tag engraved with the bible verse from Jeremiah 29:11 that stated, "For I know the plans I have for you, plans to prosper you, not to harm you, plans to give you hope and a future." I clung to this verse as I slowly closed my eyes that night, remembering the love that I had received from those two individuals who God had brought to Lake Christy especially for me. God did in fact have plans for me, plans for hope and a future. Thankfully, that was not the last time I would see these two people who changed my life that special day.

-8-
The Wait Is Over

A few weeks passed. With each passing day, my hopes of seeing Mrs. Pam and Mr. Mac again were fading. I continued to pray in an attempt to keep my protective wall from resurfacing. Trying to remain hopeful when life had been so full of trauma and disappointment was extremely challenging.

I was clinging onto the memories of Mr. Mac and Mrs. Pam. I visualized their smiles in a hope to keep that day permanently etched in my mind. I vividly remembered the warmth of their hands as they held mine and still smelled the floral perfume that Pam was wearing. However, with each passing day, my hope and smile faded. Once again, feelings of doubt and frustration plagued me. Jeremiah 29 stated that God had a plan for my future, so where was it? Just as I was on the brink of giving up hope, Mrs. Deborah transported us to her office at the Department of Social Services. Past experiences had shown me that every time we were taken to her office, change was coming. I assumed that we were relocating to yet another foster home since our behavior had been questionable in our current home.

Mrs. Deborah asked Brian and me to sit down and handed us a small booklet with pictures on the front. I assumed that we were about to be lectured in some way about how we were moving again. I mentally prepared myself to utilize one of my perfected techniques of appearing as though I was listening while blocking out the words that brought me pain. However, as my eyes scanned the booklet, I was in total shock. The smiling faces of Mrs. Pam and Mr. Mac stared at me from the cover of the book in my hands. Mrs. Deborah shared the news that they were interested in getting to know us better to possibly adopt us. My entire body was overcome with joy and sheer excitement. I began repeatedly cheering, "They are going to adopt us! They are going to adopt us!" Mrs. Deborah encouraged us to calm down long enough to look through the profile booklet that explained their story. It showed pictures of their family, friends, pets, and house. Most importantly I saw pictures of a couple who were ready to open their hearts and home to us. My thoughts had turned from fear and frustration to hope. My thoughts once again changed, "Could it be that my roller coaster journey was going to come to an end?" I was terrified to let myself believe that it was even a possibility. I had been disappointed too many times. I somehow managed to allow this news to be the glimmer of hope for which I had been anxiously awaiting.

When returning to my foster home, I happily reported to my foster parent that we had a family who was interested in adopting us. She immediately responded in her typical cruel manner by stating, "They don't want to adopt you." This time, I was able to ignore her; I knew in the depths of my heart that I was on my way to my forever family. I glanced again at my dog tag from the day we met Mrs. Pam and Mr. Mac and knew in that moment that she was wrong.

The date was set; we were scheduled to spend the day with our potential adoptive parents the following Wednesday. The hope was that we would spend the day together, and they would still want to pursue adoption after this one-on-one time. I began to count down the days and could think of little else. Each night I gripped my dog tag and repeated the verse, "For I know the plans I have for you, plans to prosper you, not to harm you, plans to give you hope and a future." I felt certain that this was a message sent to me to help me remain hopeful.

The day finally arrived. I could hardly contain my excitement. I anxiously looked out the window and waited for Mrs. Deborah. I literally threw open the screen door, ran outside, and hopped into the car at record speed. Mrs. Deborah spent the car ride trying to calm Brian and me and reminding us that we would need to be on our best behavior while spending time with our potential adoptive family.

We met Mrs. Pam and Mr. Mac at the local bookstore. I was flooded with so many conflicting emotions as we pulled into the parking lot. I was wondering, "Would they remember us? Would they still like us? Would they hurt us? Could we trust them?" Most importantly I was wondering if this could possibly be the forever family that I had been craving in the depths of my soul for so long.

As I exited the car, I immediately spotted the big, loving man with his warm and welcoming eyes. Instinct took over, and I ran to him. Without saying a word, I climbed him like a tree. He grasped me and held me for what seemed like an eternity while Mrs. Pam greeted Brian with her soothing voice and loving hug. Despite my fears, they remembered us and the connection felt the same as when we were together a Lake Christy. My dreams were coming true. I wish I could say that this was the perfect moment, but in all honesty, doubt flooded over me to the point that I felt somewhat paralyzed. More thoughts caused by previous experiences flooded my mind, "Could I really trust that these people were going to welcome us into their home? Would they make us leave when they found out who we really were and what we had really done?" Only time would tell if they would learn about my past. I reminded myself that our secrets must never be revealed.

We enjoyed an amazing day together as we played "castle" at the local park. We pretended that Mrs. Pam and Mr. Mac were the king and queen of the castle. Brian and I were the knights who were assigned to protect the king and queen from the fearsome dragon. These hours filled with fantasy and laughter were some I will never forget. Mrs.

Pam and Mr. Mac climbed with us, chased us, and shared every moment with us.

After a few joyful hours at the park, we headed to the local bowling alley. Brian and I had never set foot in a bowling alley, so I required a great deal of hands-on instruction as I learned how to knock down the pins that were waiting at the end of the lane. Mrs. Pam and Mr. Mac encouraged me and praised my efforts even when I failed. They were very willing to give as many hugs as I requested. I made certain to be on my very best behavior as I felt tremendous pressure to make them like me.

We concluded our day with an unforgettable meal at a local steakhouse. Brian and I had seen this restaurant many times, but we had only ever eaten fast food. Therefore, this experience was another first that we were able to share with Mrs. Pam and Mr. Mac. I remember Mrs. Pam's look of complete shock as she watched us consume enough food to feed several grown men. We ate salad, bread, steak, mushrooms, and a baked potato that was overloaded with cheese, butter, sour cream, and bacon. We felt like a family. I had always heard about families talking, playing, and sharing together. In this moment, I caught a glimpse of what my future might hold, a glimpse of what I would feel like if I had a true family.

As our meal came to an end, I felt myself becoming anxious. My activity level increased since I did not know what to do with the emotions that were invading. I knew that they were leaving and had no concept as to when we would see them again. Even though they assured us otherwise, I also toyed with the horrible thought that maybe they were no longer interested in adopting us. I feared that we may have misbehaved or eaten too much food at dinner and that maybe they no longer wanted us.

I later found out that my fears were unfounded; Mrs. Pam and Mr. Mac informed Mrs. Deborah at the conclusion of that visit that they wanted to become our forever family. They apparently wanted us to come HOME as soon as possible! When Mrs. Deborah delivered this news, I felt every muscle in my body begin to relax and slipped into a dreamlike state. All I had ever wanted was a family to call my own. The words and feelings did not seem real. Since we had been working in therapy on the concept of adoption for many months, I understood that this move would theoretically be our last move. Even though it seemed unreal, my nightmare was ending.

We were told that we would be moving to our adoptive home in five days. This seemed like an eternity. I immediately grabbed my personal belongings which included a few broken happy meal toys and some tattered clothing. I shoved them into a grocery bag and was ready to go. My foster parent harshly scolded me and told me to unpack my belongings since I had four days remaining. I did not care what she said at that point; I had already moved on in my mind. I stared at the ceiling that night as I battled insomnia. My mind raced with thoughts of hope and happiness for the first time in my life. In only a few short days, I would be moving to my forever home. I finally slipped into a very surface level sleep as I twisted the chain from the dog tag that had become my symbol of hope.

-9-
Going HOME?

My foot tapped the floor at a furious pace as I sat in the living room watching out the window for Mrs. Deborah. Today was the day scheduled for our move to our new home. While I was still extremely excited, I had some more doubts that had formed in my mind over the past couple of days. These doubts were emerging based on the way my social worker had changed the way she spoke of this move. Initially, she had called it a pre-adoptive placement and utilized words such as permanent, forever, and adoption. I noticed that during the last two conversations with her, she referred to it as a longer-term placement. However, she was no longer including the word adoption. Over the years, I learned to become keenly aware of what people around me were saying. While I was only eight years old, I had become a master at identification of subtle differences in language usage, body language, and other nonverbal cues. I had been forced to develop these detective skills in order to remain aware of what was happening around me. It was a safety strategy. Something had changed in the way that Mrs. Deborah presented our new situation. Despite my fears that she may not arrive to take us to our new home, she pulled into the driveway. I felt an immediate sense of relief. My doubt turned again to excitement. We were ready to travel to our new home where Mrs. Pam and Mr. Mac awaited our arrival.

The car ride seemed like an eternity. I used all of my self control to keep from persistently uttering the stereotypical words, "Are we there yet?" As we got closer, I heard Mrs. Deborah call Mrs. Pam to tell her that we were only 10 minutes away. I could hardly wait; the anticipation was killing me. While I was still not convinced that this placement would be permanent, my confidence that these people wanted us and were eagerly awaiting our arrival began to build.

As we pulled into the driveway, I looked up in complete amazement at what seemed to be a brick mansion. This was by far the largest house I had ever seen. Mrs. Pam and Mr. Mac must have been watching for us because they opened the front door with smiles before we even had a chance to get out of the car. I grabbed my tattered bin of pathetic items from the car and immediately ran to the door. All of my belongings were packed into one broken bin that contained a few cracked happy meal toys and a few shirts that were either stained or torn. While the state of my belongings was pitiful, they were mine. I wanted to ensure their safe delivery, so I was sure to keep them in my line of sight. I placed them on the floor at my feet and received a greeting of the most comforting hugs I had ever felt. We also immediately caught a whiff of some food that brought an immediate sense of comfort. The house smelled of warmth and kindness. I will never forget that smell. It was Mrs. Pam's homemade chicken tortilla soup. I was distracted by the smell and wanted to eat, but I first needed to explore my new surroundings and make sure my things were safe.

The living room was a large, open space with one huge couch for the entire family to share. Warm, cozy blankets were placed on the couch and painted pictures in my head of snuggling up with my new family. The kitchen was open and looked directly into the living room; it was covered with beautiful decorations, spices, and other items that made me feel a sense of welcome. Naturally, I was eager to see my bedroom. As we went up the stairs, I caught glimpses of family photos throughout the house. This was not a house, this was a true home.

I entered my room with great anticipation. I saw clearly that Mrs. Pam and Mr. Mac had prepared this room just for me based on conversation during our last visit. I had mentioned that I liked G.I. Joe. I was amazed; not only did they remember that conversation, but they had decorated my room with G.I.Joe posters, toys, and matching bedding. These actions dealt major blows to the doubts that had been a part of me for so long. This was all for me! I was not invisible for the first time in my life. Brian giggled with utter joy as he learned that his room was connected to mine by a shared bathroom. His room was filled with jungle animals, including a five-foot stuffed giraffe, to welcome him. In addition to our bedrooms, a large bonus room was set up as a play room with a game system, television, and more puzzles and games than I ever knew existed.

My internal dialogue was taking a more positive tone as I asked myself, "Is this really my home?" I was not accustomed to these positive emotions and felt very overwhelmed. It was almost too much to handle. I did not allow myself to embrace the hope and immediately heard the negative thoughts returning with a vengeance, "Don't get too excited because you are going to lose all of this. These people don't really want you. Wait until they find out your secrets. You don't deserve any of this." I pretended that I was not terrified to open my heart and trust Mrs. Pam and Mr. Mac who seemed to have the best of intentions. They seemed like wonderful people, but I wondered, "What would make them different from all the others who let me down?" Only time would answer my burning question. I felt a huge sense of relief as I watched Mrs. Deborah drive away. Watching her car leave my line of sight assured me that I would remain with this family, at least for the moment.

That night, both Mrs. Pam and Mr. Mac came to tuck me into my new bed. All of this attention was welcomed but overwhelming. They noticed that I was afraid, so they shared comforting words, a bedtime story, and a prayer. Mr. Mac sang a song that I will never forget as long as I live. He shared with me that his father had sung the Marine Corps Hymn to him as a child. This giant, muscle-bound man made himself completely vulnerable and sang from his heart in order to provide me a few moments of comfort. I tucked myself deeply into my blankets as I had always done in the past, but this time I felt safe. Both Mrs. Pam and Mr. Mac remained in my room by my side until I fell soundly asleep. This place was a dream come true.

_10_

Settling In

Over the next few weeks, Brian and I began to settle into our new environment. Each day was better than the previous day as we learned more about the people that we hoped and prayed would someday become our family. We met many people, including Mrs. Pam's parents. When we met her parents, I immediately saw where she had learned her kind and warm-hearted ways. Mrs. Pam's parents, Art and Mary, immediately embraced us as their own grandchildren and spoiled us with love and kindness. Mrs. Pam and Mr. Mac also introduced us to neighbors, church members, and more family friends than I can recall. Every single person welcomed us with open arms. This soothed my wounded heart. This was a different world than the one I had previously known; this was a world where people seemed to genuinely care the second that they met me. They seemed to love me simply because they loved Mrs. Pam and Mr. Mac.

Although Brian and I had absolutely no concept of how a family was supposed to function, we began to develop some family routines. We learned the rules and expectations as well as the rewards and consequences. Knowing exactly what to expect at all times created a sense of safety and security for me. I was comforted by the consistency in knowing that the same reward or consequence would happen each and every time. Mrs. Pam and Mr. Mac established new rules around the consumption of food. We had never had access to such a vast array of foods, including fruits and vegetables. The healthy foods tasted amazing and seemed to be filling previously unmet nutritional needs. My brother and I would literally eat until we were uncomfortably full and bordering on sick. Since I had limited food in the past, it was nearly impossible to let go of the fear that my present food supply may disappear. With each meal we feared that it would be our last, remembering that our past was so filled with sudden and unexpected changes.

As time passed, I felt my protective wall slowly being chipped away by these adults who were consistently meeting our basic needs as well as providing love and affection and a level of acceptance that felt new to us. By the second week, I decided to test the emotional waters by calling Mrs. Pam, "Mom", during a casual conversation. We had never discussed this issue, but I so desperately wanted it to become true. I looked her way and said, "Hey, Mom, can I get a snack?" While she looked somewhat shocked, a very clear smile appeared on her face. She looked simply delighted and continued on with the conversation as if nothing was out of the ordinary. I clearly understood that this term was acceptable and welcomed. From that day forward, Mr. Mac and Mrs. Pam became Dad and Mom.

During the first few weeks, Mom, Dad, Brian, and I spent a great deal of time bonding as a family. We explored museums, learned to play new games, watched movies, and enjoyed very lengthy and detailed conversations. Bedtime became our daily "check in time." We processed our day, talked about the good and the bad, and shared thoughts and feelings. With each day, I grew more comfortable with our conversations; I felt my wall crumbling as I safely exposed my heart for the first time in my life.

Since we were placed in a new home, the Department of Social Services approved a delay in our start of school in order to adjust to our new setting. After a few weeks of straight family time, we returned to school. My mom taught a preschool class for children with autism at a local school. Fortunately for us, she made arrangements for us to attend the same school. I gained a great sense of comfort in knowing that Mom was literally a few steps down the hall if I needed her.

As I entered yet another new classroom, I immediately discovered that I was behind academically. Since I had been through four different schools and multiple homes, my delay in academic skills came as no shock to anyone. I had spent the last four years focused on meeting my basic safety and survival needs; academics had clearly not been a priority in my life. A team at the school explained to my mom that I would always struggle academically; they said I may never succeed in the school setting.

My mom left that meeting visibly angry and determined to prove them wrong. Since she was a trained teacher, she immediately began to help me work on the skills that appeared to be missing. I sensed the fire in her and knew that I would get the help that I so desperately required. We spent every free moment working on math and reading skills. She found a way to make learning fun and built my self esteem over time. Time and effort proved that the school officials were incorrect. I was working above grade level within 2 years. I continued to work and succeed far above grade level. To this day, my mom makes sure the the school officials are aware of my continued success. She shares this information not to boast but to serve as a friendly reminder that adults can never predict future success for a child.

In addition to school, Brian and I began taking a mixed martial arts class which was taught by my dad and a close family friend, Kevin Hunt who owned the school. This served as a great release. We participated two nights per week. I quickly learned new ways to express my anger and frustration. I had been on my very best behavior since arriving. This period of behavior is often called the "honeymoon period." Over the years I had learned to charm the adults in my life in an effort to ensure food and safety. My worst fear was ending up back in the foster care system, so I did my best to please everyone around me despite my lingering fears.

-11-
Fear of the Unknown Again

As I mentioned previously, I had been forced to become constantly aware of what was being said and done around me at all times. I often appeared to be engaged in an activity of some sort, but ultimately I was on constant watch. This hypervigilant state became exhausting, but it was something I had learned to do from a very early age. As I became more familiar with my new parents, I studied their reactions, body language, tone of voice, and how they dealt with various emotions.

About a month after Brian and I had been placed in our new home, I sensed a change. I noticed an increase in the phone calls that caused Mom and Dad to step outside so that we would not hear the conversation. The whispers increased, and Mom and Dad seemed to be having more private conversations. I had become very tightly bonded to my mom and had developed the skills to easily read her underlying emotions despite her best efforts to disguise them. My anxiety began to increase as I noticed a distressed look that remained on her face nearly constantly. Both Mom and Dad appeared to be more short-tempered and anxious. I knew something big was about to happen, so I heightened my alertness even more. Those old familiar feelings of fear were creeping back into my thoughts.

One stormy afternoon, my mom was absent from the living room for quite an extended period of time. Out of concern, I searched for her. I heard some noise in her bathroom, and instinct took over as I opened the door without knocking. In that moment, I witnessed the woman who had become my protector, caregiver, and nurturer curled in a ball on the bathroom floor with tears flowing from her pained brown eyes. In shock and feeling afraid, I continued to watch and listen as I heard her offer a prayer. She was pleading with God for patience and understanding in this difficult situation. Hearing her words caused a flood of fears: "What was she referring to? Were we leaving again?" Watching her cry pained me very deeply. I had never been connected enough to any other human being to feel emotional pain simply because they were suffering. Every ounce of hope that I had was immediately put into question. Although I was small and I felt weak in the knees, I dropped to the floor to hold her in my arms just as she had done for me so many times.

A few moments later, Dad called a family meeting. At this point, I felt as if I might as well go and pack my bags. I felt certain I was about to lose the only good thing that ever happened in my life. Mom and Dad sat us down and explained to the best of their ability that they wanted to have us stay with them forever but that certain things needed to happen in court for this to occur. They explained with tears in their eyes that we needed to wait, hope, and pray. Although I had no idea at the time, my mom and dad were warned by social workers that there was a 50 percent chance that we would end up back in the foster care system. The courts wanted to allow our birth parents more time to correct their actions in an attempt to reunify our birth family despite their repeated failures. Apparently four years had not been long enough in the eyes of the court system. I had no idea that Mrs. Pam and Mr. Mac, who I viewed as my only true Mom and Dad, were about to enter a very lengthy court battle to fight on our behalf.

This news immediately struck panic in my heart. I had become accustomed to moving from home to home. However, this time, I had been told that I would remain here forever. As a result, I had let these amazing people into my heart and soul. I could not fathom the thought of leaving what had become my home. I immediately began to rebuild my protective wall that I had begun to dismantle over the last month; I felt certain I was going to lose the only people whom I loved.

The next eight months were filled with a tremendous amount of uncertainty. I felt myself again being slowly overtaken by fear, anxiety, and eventually anger. My brother and I became fearful that someone would come and take us away, so we systematically locked all of the doors in the house. We accidentally locked our family out of the house on a number of occasions. Hypervigilance had returned, and we remained very aware of our surroundings. I was keenly aware of every phone call, conversation and email. While Mom and Dad tried to the best of their ability to ease our fears, they could find no words that assured us that we were not going to be taken away. Brian began to hoard food in anticipation of being removed from our forever home; he felt as though he needed to start planning for the future which would likely involve us going hungry again.

Each month our social worker was required to come for a visit. In the past, she had been the one to deliver the news of change. Although we loved her very much, we dreaded her visits and exhibited a concerning level of anxiety days before each one. I began having nightly panic attacks as her visits approached. We felt certain that she would ask us to pack our items and go with her. I was determined not to allow this to happen, not again. Our new family unit eventually worked out a system that put Brian and me at ease. The plan included the presence of my grandmother, Pam's mom, during our monthly social worker visits. She then took Brian and me out for ice cream while the social worker visited with Mom and Dad. Pulling out of the driveway with our grandmother meant that we were not leaving with Mrs. Deborah.

As time passed, the anxiety was clearly building with Mom and Dad. They were having very lengthy phone conversations with attorneys, Guardian Ad Litem's, social workers, and therapists. They took occasional day trips to Craven County to meet with attorneys. My fear was building like never before. I began to act out behaviorally. I felt certain that I was going to lose this family that I felt was a true gift from God. In order to protect myself emotionally, I decided that I would act out in order to get Mrs. Pam and Mr. Mac to send me away. That way the loss would be my fault, and I would not feel the pain when removed. Although I am now ashamed of my actions, I became very angry and difficult to manage during this time. I often lashed out and said hurtful things in order to push my family away before I lost them. I often refused to do what was asked of me as an act of rebellion. I walked around with an angry scowl while wearing a black hoodie that I could pull over my face. I felt safer hiding under the hood. For the first time, I began to question God's plan for my life. Why would God allow me to go through so much adversity? I felt that I must have done something wrong to deserve all of this pain.

Thankfully, my plan to push away my family that I had grown to love so deeply was not effective. My mom had a background in behavior management, psychology, and child development. She had also done extensive study on how to help children who had experienced trauma. Mom and Dad literally invested every moment into my brother and me. They were determined to break down my wall that was now seemingly impenetrable. We spent extensive time in therapy and read many books together. They also spent time teaching me to identify my own triggers. Triggers were sights, sounds, smells, actions, or items in my environment that caused me to remember traumatic events. Instead of responding to my anger with punishment, Mom and Dad helped me to identify the reasons behind my feelings. They helped me develop ways to manage them appropriately. We threw rocks into the river, ran on the treadmill, punched a punching bag, and wrote in a journal as needed.

Although I was nine years old, I deeply craved physical affection. I was in constant need of hugs. My mom allowed me to climb on her lap in the rocking chair and held me tightly in her arms and calmed me at least once a day for a span of 6 months or more; this helped to ease my tumultuous feelings. I was angry about my past. I was even more livid that I finally had a family to love me and I had to live each day with the fear of losing them. The difference from past experiences was that I had a group of people to help me understand my anger and help me process through it. We were Team Taylor.

The agony of the unknown seemed to linger indefinitely. Court hearings continued, social workers took vacations, important papers remained untouched on desks, and no one, except for our new family, seemed to care that we desired nothing more than the security in knowing that we were home to stay. Frustrations mounted as we continued to wait for our fate to be determined. Dealing with so much uncertainty actually forged an unbreakable bond among our family. We learned to speak very openly and approach our fears as a family unit through prayer. We also sought comfort from our church family as we waited. We were already a family in our hearts, despite what the judge would say. We were becoming stronger every day, but the deep dark secrets housed in the depths of my mind threatened our newly found strength. The time had come to reveal the secrets that had been destroying me for years.

-12-
Secrets Revealed

I had spent my entire life keeping secrets that were so horrific that they were literally eating away at my soul. I carried these secrets for so long because I had never developed the ability to trust anyone in my life. My new mom, Pam, had proven time and time again that she could be trusted and loved me no matter what I revealed. Unconditional love was clear and felt for the first time in my life. Her actions finally made it possible to unload the heavy baggage that I had carried for so long. Mom and Dad had heard all the gruesome details about my past neglect and exposure to domestic violence, but they had never heard the details that I needed to expose about my secrets.

As Mom was tucking me into my cozy bed, my heart was pounding so hard that I felt certain that she could hear it. I felt as if I could not breathe, but knew that I had to push through the pain and share my entire life with her. She was my mom. I reached out for her hand as I often did and looked into her warm face and said, "I have something I need to tell you, but I am not sure you can love me anymore." She sat on the floor, tightly grasped my hand, and began to listen attentively while she assured me that nothing I would say could change her love for me. Those words were the final push I needed to let go of everything that I was carrying.

For the next hour, I shared horrific details about sexual abuse that I had suffered from the age of two years old. I had never shared these details with anyone because I was living in sheer terror. My biological uncle on my birth father's side, Lester, began sexually abusing my older brother, Travis, and me when I was a toddler. Instead of protecting and guiding us as an uncle should do, he committed unspeakable acts that damaged us to the core. Without intervention, those who have been abused often become abusers. This vicious cycle was demonstrated in my birth family. My older brother sexually abused my sister and me for many years until we were separated and placed into different foster homes. I shared with my mom very graphic details about the horror I had been experiencing throughout my entire life. I also shared with Mom that my birth parents were aware of the abuse and permitted it to continue and refused to get us help. As I shared details with Mom, I buried my head deeply under the pillows and was unable to look her in the face. This was, without question, one of the most difficult moments of my life. I was so filled with rage, sadness, guilt, shame, and utter terror as I shared every memory. The tears flowed, and I kept uttering the phrase, "How can you love me?" My mom's face was flooded with tears as she held me tightly. Just as she always did, she reached out to me and held me in her arms for over an hour. I will never forget her words, "It's not your fault; you were a child." She comforted me by repeatedly forcing me to look her in the eyes as she told me how much she loved me and that she and Dad would help me through this. After more than two hours of an indescribable surge of emotion, six years worth of tension melted from my body because I no longer had to carry this burden in isolation. While I had NEVER continued the cycle by sexually abusing others, I did carry a tremendous amount of guilt and shame from the abuse I had experienced. Simply by sharing this burden, I felt as though a thousand pound weight had been lifted from my shame filled mind. As this weight lifted, I felt the healing beginning in my heart; it was time to heal.

-13-
Let the Healing Begin

In recent years, I have learned that an open wound is highly painful as it begins to heal. This extreme pain is partly caused by the restoration of the nerve endings that have been damaged. With the return of feeling, pain returns. The complete healing of the wound is not possible without the healing of the nerves. Therefore, the healing process can be quite painful.

The healing process surrounding my abuse was very similar. I had many deep emotional wounds. A successful healing process demanded that I feel the deep pain associated with each and every hurtful bit of emotional damage that had been inflicted over the years. True healing required me to expose the wounds and feel the pain in order for healing to occur.

After sharing my deepest secrets with my mom and dad, I felt a total sense of relief and freedom. Although discussing my abuse was extremely painful, I was beginning to understand that this was the only way to complete the healing process that began the moment I moved to my new home. These days were some of the darkest days of my life, but my family was able to pull me into the light. In addition to my family, I also clung to my hope in God with new fervor. I invested time in prayer and developed a true understanding that God and my new parents truly loved me unconditionally. In the light of this new unconditional love, I developed a deep, strong desire to change and move beyond the trauma of my past. I was eager to put in the work and endure the necessary torture that came with processing my past in order to move to a brighter future. My parents walked beside me during every step of this journey of healing that included extensive therapy, accessing and reading as many resources as possible, frequent lengthy conversations, and more hugs and comforting words than can be imagined by the common person.

I initially felt a tremendous amount of guilt and shame. Over time, I learned that the abuse was not my fault; I had been a young child with no understanding of sexuality and no ability to keep adults from hurting me. As most children do, I had an innate desire to respect and please the adults around me. I was the perfect victim, a child who felt invisible and helpless. In my mind no greater betrayal exists than when an adult utilizes their power to abuse a child. I was powerless at the hands of my abusers.

Mom and Dad taught me many new skills to deal with my emotions. I learned to easily identify triggers and handle them as needed. My parents stressed repeatedly and proved daily that this journey was one that they would take along with me. As a result, I no longer felt alone. We fought the battle hard each and every day. Although a clear victory took considerable time, my self-description eventually changed from "victim" to "survivor".

Exposing the most painful part of my past in this book was not an easy decision for me. My fear was that I would become a victim of ignorance and judgement. I still fear that others will look at me differently. I worry that others might think that I will be a perpetrator because of the abuse I suffered. **I have never and will never act out sexually toward another.** I was given a forensic evaluation that determined that I have never been at any risk of acting out sexually. Not only will I NEVER act out toward another individual, but I am planning to devote my life to ensuring that this does not happen to other children. A common stereotype states that those who experience sexual abuse will become sexually active at a younger age. However, I am now a strong, Christian young man with a clear understanding of how God designed sex. God makes all things new. Therefore, I proudly wear a purity ring on a chain around my neck to symbolize my promise to wait until marriage to enjoy sex as God designed it. After much discussion, thought and prayer, I have come to the conclusion that if someone is going to ignorantly judge me for something that was not my fault, then that person is someone that I do not need or want in my life. I do recognize that without help and healing, significant damage can occur as a result of abuse. However, I want others to know that healing is more than possible; I have actually proven it true. While I will always feel pain from my past events to some extent, I have been able to heal and am learning to live a very successful life filled with hope and joy. Healing these painful wounds is the hardest thing I have ever done, but it is worth every surge of anger, all the tears, and every sleepless night. I am no longer a victim; I am a survivor. I am strong and plan to help others throughout my life.

Our society tries to ignore the fact that 1 in 10 children will face some form of sexual abuse before their eighteenth birthday. The statistics are even more alarming within the foster care system where 75-80 percent of the children have experienced sexual abuse. The time has come to bravely and openly talk about it so that children are not forced to suffer in silence as I did for so long. I am breaking that silence through this story of my life. The silence is what causes the pain. After extensive study, I have learned that many individuals carry the pain of sexual abuse into adulthood. My hope is that I can help others free themselves of this tremendous pain and suffering and move forward to live the life that they deserve.

While memories from my past still hurt at times, I have successfully navigated the various stages of healing with tremendous help and support. I have fully grasped the fact that the fault for my abuse is not mine. I am no longer an abuse victim. I am a strong,

Christian young man who is looking at my future and not my past. I have fully submitted my life to God and plan to allow Him to use what has happened to me to change the lives of others.

-14-
"You Can't Fix Stupid"

Although I was able to begin healing from my horrific abuse, I still feared the possibility of being removed from this family who had pulled me out of the darkness. While we waited on judges, lawyers, therapists, social workers and others, my fear intensified.

Almost 13 months after Brian and I arrived at our new home, Mom and Dad received word that our court hearing was scheduled for mid-September. Because this court hearing would decide if my birth parents would lose all legal rights to my siblings and me or be awarded more time to comply with the recommendations of social services, it was called the "Termination of Parental Rights." At the end of this court hearing. Brian and I would either be permanently awarded to our new mom and dad to become a forever family, or we would re-enter the foster care system. This one hearing would determine my fate. While I had been anxiously awaiting this news, I felt an utter sense of terror when I heard that it had actually been scheduled. I got sick to my stomach just thinking about the possible outcomes.

Mom and dad spent endless hours preparing documents and presentations. In addition to taking the stand as a foster parent, Mom had also been called as an expert witness in the case due to her background and training in child development and behavior. Both Mom and Dad were prepared to fight for us and longed for the opportunity to speak on our behalf.

Because the court hearing was scheduled to take place in the Craven County Courthouse which was located over three hours away from home, Mom and Dad also worked out arrangements for the care of Brian and me during the court sessions. We were not permitted in the courtroom, so they planned for us to stay in locations nearby; they wanted to see us each night after court. Friends and family offered to help us during this time of chaos and uncertainty. Dad's parents traveled from Maryland to North Carolina to keep Brian busy at a nearby beach house. The Harris family, close family friends, owned a house about 20 minutes from the courthouse. They prepared to keep me each day. Mom and Dad planned to keep us distracted while they joined our grandmother, Mary (Pam's Mom), and close family friends, Brent and Kathy Powers, to battle in court during the day. My grandfather, Art, remained at home so that he could tend to our animals while we were gone.

Mom and Dad were told that the court hearing would probably take five days or longer, so they helped Brian and me pack our bags to stay as long as needed. The night before we left, we gathered at the home of our Pastor, Dexter Richardson, where we spent very emotional time in prayer with many friends and family. They prayed for God to give us strength during the court hearing and for patience and understanding to accept whatever decision was made. I grasped onto my dog tag that was engraved with what had become my favorite bible verse. I carried it everywhere with me. My mom was in tears much of the evening. I tried to comfort her as she had comforted me over the past year. When we finally crawled into our beds, the looming court decisions made it impossible for any of us to sleep. We woke up very early the next morning, loaded our van with a variety of items that we might need during the court proceedings, and traveled to Craven County for the court sessions that would change my life one way or another.

On the first morning of the court hearings, Mom and Dad gathered Brian and me around them as a family. We tightly grasped hands together as we prayed in preparation for a very emotional and challenging day. I saw the familiar, distressed look on Mom's face. I reached up with my small hand to wipe tears from her face. In an attempt to offer additional comfort, I reached around my neck, removed my cherished dog tag, gave it to her, and told her to carry it with her for good luck. She immediately placed it around her neck and embraced me with a big hug.

When Mom and Dad dropped me off at the Harris' home, I felt like my arms and legs were made of rubber. The Harris family welcomed me with open arms and immediately began to distract me with toys and games. I appreciated their efforts, but nothing was able to tear me away from my thoughts of what might have been happening in the courtroom. I knew that Mom and Dad would be confronted by members of my birth family. Many of them were unstable emotionally and had a history of violence. While I knew that Mom and Dad were strong enough to protect themselves, part of me was ashamed that they would see and experience this part of my past.

Throughout the day, I busied myself at the beach and tried to keep my thoughts away from the courtroom. I constantly watched the clock while hoping that Mom and Dad would come back with good news. At 5:23 in the afternoon, they pulled into the gravel driveway to retrieve me. The looks on their faces immediately told me that they had not received good news that day. They reminded me that this process would likely take several days. Without providing too much detail, they explained that some people had gotten out of control during the court hearing. Mom and Dad had been escorted to their vehicle after court by the police to ensure their safety. I wish I could say that I was shocked, but this news came as no surprise. I had often witnessed unexplainable behaviors from various members of my birth family in the past. Every ounce of me wished that I could do something to protect Mom and Dad from my birth family, but I could do nothing.

Three more days of grueling court sessions passed. The daily emotional turmoil of this process was tiring for each of us. When Mom and Dad arrived to pick us up at the conclusion of the fourth day, they informed us that the judge would be making his final decision the following day. We had only one more day until we discovered our fate. That night was the longest of my life. My family spent much time in prayer. We clung to our little family unit, hoping that the decision that would be made the following day would make our family permanent. Somehow, amidst turmoil and craziness, we managed to find a sense of peace as we clung to one another. We closed our eyes that night knowing that our fate would be sealed the following day as one man made his decision based on four days of testimony.

As Mom and Dad prepared for the final day in court, I saw a look of sheer exhaustion on their faces. Mom put on a beautiful black and white dress and placed the dog tag carefully around her neck once again. She had worn it to court each and every day. She told me that she looked at it frequently throughout the trial to remind her that God was in control. We each clung to the verse that had been given to us more than18 months earlier when we met at Lake Christy. It reminded us that God had a plan for our family from the very start. While we were very concerned, we felt certain that our faith would be rewarded with a final judgement in our favor.

Throughout that final day of court, I watched the hands slowly move around the clock. I attempted to busy myself by playing with some GI Joe action figures with my friends, Logan and Savanna. I tried to hide my anxiety, but my thoughts were racing like an uncontrolled tornado. Finally, I heard the van throwing rocks in the gravel as it approached. I had planned to read the expression on the faces of Mom and Dad before they stepped out of the car. I wanted to see if I could gain information about the outcome before they reached the door. All of my hopes and dreams were hanging on this one moment. I was not able to decipher this nonverbal information until they walked up the steps. They exuded a look of sheer exhaustion, but they also seemed to have a sense of great peace. I saw it on my mom's face. The distressed look from the morning has been transformed into relief.

As they entered the house, they asked Brian and me to head to the bedroom so that we could have a private discussion. That suggestion scared me. Questions began to scream in my mind, "If it was good news, why did they not tell me the minute they walked through the door? What were they waiting for?" The second we crossed into the bedroom my mom screamed, "The judge said yes!" I literally leaped for joy into my mother's loving arms, then launched into a crazy rampage around the room that included laughter, jumping on the bed, rolling on the floor, and screaming for joy. This was a celebration like no other. I was free at last from the chains that bound me to my past. Finally, I could be legally adopted by the two individuals who had already become my mom and dad.

As we ate a celebratory meal, we talked over the events of the day. Once again, Mom and Dad spared us from the details regarding our birth family. However, they did share one fact about my maternal birth grandmother, Lilith. She had an extensive history of misbehavior in the courtroom and had a documented history of significant mental illness, including religious delusions. In my opinion, she had grossly misused religion to lead my birth family in a cult-like manner for many years. I was not shocked when my family reported that Lilith became violent when the final verdict was delivered. She quickly approached my new grandmother, Mary, and reached her hands toward her shoulder. The baliff in the courtroom quickly intervened to disrupt any physical harm. The baliff was almost forced to taze her and required her to remain against the wall until the hearing was concluded.

For obvious safety reasons, the baliff escorted my parents to the car after the court hearing. She shared a final comment with them that still resonates with us. She said, "You can't fix stupid, but you sure can taze it!"

-15-
What's in A Name?

Since the hurdle of court was completed, we could finally await our adoption without the fear of losing the people who had become so dear to us. This required even more waiting. I felt like my entire life had been spent waiting on other people to determine my future. Knowing that this would be the final step made the waiting somewhat easier to handle.

During the wait, Brian and I became very interested in a show called *Adoption Stories*. Since the subject matter of this show resonated with me on a personal level, I watched this as much as possible. As I watched stories with happy endings, I hoped that my special adoption day would soon arrive.

I began to notice that many of the children talked about wanting a fresh start and a new beginning. A few of the stories highlighted the fact that children were able to change their names upon adoption. I always knew that my last name would change, but I had never once considered the possibility of changing my first name. I immediately knew that this was the right decision for me. I approached Mom and Dad with the idea, hoping that they would embrace my plan. While they were supportive, they wanted to be sure that I had adequately thought through this life-changing decision. After weeks of discussion with my therapist, I decided to pick a new name in commemoration of my new start in life.

Picking a new name was quite a daunting task. I began to search the internet for random names that sounded good to me. One afternoon, Mom approached me with a name book and suggested that I pick a name that was meaningful. She suggested that I look up the meanings behind the names to help with my selection. She left me alone on the porch with a huge book of names and their corresponding definitions. After nearly three hours, I narrowed it down to three possibilities. When I read them to my family, they all unanimously agreed that one stood out among the rest: Trent. The definitions of the name Trent vary from book to book. Our particular resource defined the name Trent as "one who is strong and overcomes." Due to the support of my new family and friends, I was beginning to feel strong, like someone who could overcome adversity. This name was a perfect fit. After selecting a first name, I then needed to select a new middle name. This decision was simple. I chose to take the name, McLeod. This was my future adoptive father's middle name. The final decision was made. Upon adoption, my new legal name would be Trent McLeod Taylor.

Brian also decided to change his name for the same reasons. He selected the name,

Michael, which means "Of God". He chose to be called Michael McLeod Taylor. My brother and I liked the sound of our new names. We asked people to begin calling us "Trent" and "Mike" even before the names were made official in court. My birth-given name was part of my past. I buried that name along with my past history of trauma and abuse. Because changing a name is a decision with a big impact, it requires careful consideration. While a name change is not the correct plan for all children being adopted, it was the best decision for me. The only thing left to do was await the day that we could make our names official.

-16-
Finally

My heart literally skipped a beat each and every time the phone rang. Every day was spent waiting for the phone call that would deliver the news that our adoption was final. Finally our prayers were answered. The call that changed our lives came on Monday, November 1, 2010. My dad picked up the phone and had a conversation with the clerk at the Craven County Courthouse. She asked, "When do you want to come to finalize your adoption?" Jokingly, my dad responded, "We will be there tomorrow." Thinking that we would be in for another lengthy wait, he was shocked when she responded, "We have an opening at 9:00 a.m." My dad smiled and told the clerk that we would drop everything and be there first thing in the morning. As he hung up the phone and delivered the news to

Mike and me, we jumped for joy. As in the past, questions once again flitted through my mind, "Could it possibly be? Is it really true?" However, this time the questions were answered with hope instead of fear and dread. According to the news we just received, we would officially be a family in less than 24 hours. While we had been a family in our hearts since Mike and I walked through the front door on August 25, 2009, our family unit would become official in the eyes of the law and nothing could ever change that. We would be a family forever.

Our family knew that all of us would be standing before the judge in the morning to officially stamp our adoption decree. Mike and I wanted to have the perfect attire for the momentous occasion. Mom took us on a quick trip to the mall so that we could purchase new outfits. The feelings of excitement were uncontainable. I tried on a few shirts of different colors and styles, but I finally decided on a simple, blue dress shirt. I also wanted a tie to complete my outfit. However, closing hours at the mall were approaching, and we ran out of time. Although I knew it would be too large for a nine year old boy, I pleaded to borrow a tie from Dad's collection. When we returned home, I anxiously sorted through the pile of ties to find the perfect one. I finally selected a tie that I knew was one of dad's favorites. Bedtime arrived, so I carefully laid out my clothing for the next day. Before I crawled into bed, I took one final look at the outfit and envisioned myself wearing it before the judge on my long-awaited adoption day. The rush of emotions coursing through my mind caused me to toss and turn. I kept glancing at the dog tag that was resting on my nightstand. As my eyes slowly closed, I pondered the verse that God had given to me. Tomorrow was the day that would change my future and allow God's plan to continue to unfurl.

When the loud alarm clock sounded at 5:00 a.m. the next morning, I was momentarily confused by the early wake-up call until I remembered the importance of the day. We all quickly prepared for the three-hour trip to the courthouse where our fate would be sealed. My grandparents arrived and the adults downed some coffee in order to stay awake for the drive ahead. Joining us for the special occasion was a priority for Gram and Pop; they were anticipating officially becoming our grandparents. Our close family friends, Isaac and Laura, also planned to meet us at the courthouse. While many other friends and family had planned to attend our adoption ceremony, their availability was limited due to our less-than-24-hour notice.

The ride seemed endless. As we neared our destination, I began to see familiar roads, buildings, and landmarks. As we drove through old and familiar surroundings, I was flooded with sadness, anger, and feelings of betrayal. Mom was always very in tune to my emotions and had anticipated my feelings that came as we passed through the area. She immediately reached out for my hand to offer comfort, looked deep into my eyes, and promised that this was the final trip down this painful memory lane. She began to turn the conversation to one of hope. I continued to grip her hand until we arrived at the courthouse.

The courthouse was located in the historic part of town. It was adorned by beautiful, well-established trees and buildings that were architectural wonders. Mrs. Deborah was there to greet us with a warm smile. Unlike many social workers, she had poured her heart and soul into ensuring happiness for Brian (soon to be Michael) and me. This had been a long and painful journey for her as well. Today was the culmination of many hours of fighting on our behalf. As we approached the courthouse stairs, she embraced us with tears in her eyes. She handed us a colorful bouquet of balloons, a framed photo, and a card that was filled with encouraging words and expressions of love.

Tears flooded her eyes as we gathered under a beautiful oak tree to take some photographs to commemorate this event.

As we entered the courthouse, I could not help but think about the endless hours that my mom and dad had spent in this same building fighting on our behalf. They did everything in their power to ensure that we would be a family forever. I paused for a moment to stop and reflect on the fact that these people loved us enough to voluntarily endure such distress.

We entered a small room and were asked to be seated on a large wooden bench that appeared to be an antique. It creaked as we sat down. We then waited in total silence to be called. A few minutes later, we were called to enter a small room where stacks of documents waited for us. There we learned that we would be permitted to pull the stamp down on our own official adoption decree. The stamp contraption would emboss a seal on the beautiful paper that would declare the reality of our adoption. I would have a family.

I shook with excitement. I hoped that my name would be called first; I was ready to complete this journey. My name was called, and I moved to the large metal handle. I placed both hands on the knob as my family gathered in as close as possible. With every bit of power I possessed, I pulled the handle down and heard the precious sound of the official stamp being forever imprinted on this legal document. Everyone applauded and hugged as we reveled in the long-anticipated moment. My adoption was official. My name would forever be Trent McLeod Taylor. Michael had his turn next. Because he did not have the strength needed to complete the task on his own, Mike sat on Dad's lap as they pulled the lever down together. Again, the celebrating ensued. Our family was official.

While the second day of November will always be a day of celebration, this actual adoption day was glorious beyond description. We celebrated by joining our group of extended family and friends that evening at the Brazilian Steakhouse.

We prayed in thanks to God and celebrated as toasts were made in our honor. I sat and reflected on how my life had changed. I had gone from searching the streets for food because the adults in my life were unable to care for me to sitting in a beautiful restaurant with a large group of people who loved me unconditionally. They were all there to celebrate me. Part of me still felt that I was not deserving of all that I had been given, but each time my mom and dad embraced me in a hug, I was reminded that I was loved. I was HOME!

-17-
Time to Celebrate

The social worker visits, stealthy phone calls, attorney meetings, and Guardian Ad Litem involvement were done. Slowly but surely, we began to feel a sense of normalization. Our lives had been filled with fear, worry, sadness, betrayal and disappointment for so long that we found releasing it difficult. We constantly needed to be reminded that we did not need to worry any longer. We could hardly believe that we were never leaving this home. Since our need for a reminder was so great, Mike and I had our adoption decrees framed. Each of us hung them over our bed so that we could see them each and every day.

Prior to our adoption, Mom and Dad stated that we would have a celebration of epic proportions after it was completed. Since the adoption was official, we needed to start planning what would be a party to remember. The party was scheduled for early December at a local venue that typically housed large events such as weddings, graduations, and other milestone celebrations. We created a guest list that included more than 200 friends and family. These people had provided tremendous support during the grueling and lengthy court process. We wanted to thank them. Our thank you was an invitation to this celebratory party to commemorate the official welcome of Mike and me into our forever family. As plans became more definite, our excitement grew.

On the night of the party, my excitement burst to overflowing as I entered the ballroom. I scanned the room and saw beautiful, individual Christmas trees majestically adorning each table. The trees were each filled with ornaments that had been hand-painted by my grandmother. Each ornament was in the shape of a heart and had our names on one side and the words "forever family" lovingly painted on the back. I looked down and saw M&M's at each table that had a picture of Mike and me printed on them. I had never seen a piece of candy with a picture printed on it. I felt like a star. The large stage glowed with beautiful spotlights and backlights of various colors. In the middle of the room was a small table. In the center of the ornamental table was a tall, mother-of-pearl candle that had a picture of our family on the front. True amazement filled me as I gazed at the details and effort put forth to celebrate us. My parents had thought of every loving detail possible. The band played as the guests began to arrive. I must have been hugged over 100 times that night as everyone came to celebrate with us. We enjoyed an amazing meal and spent time talking to our supportive family and friends. I knew that Mom had planned a program for the evening, but I could never have imagined what was to come. Pastor Dexter Richardson who had been with us through this entire journey offered a prayer to open the evening. Shortly after, a family friend read an emotional poem that was written by my mom called "Behind Their Smiles." Mom was entirely too emotional to read the words so she asked her friend to read on her behalf. The words in the poem were so genuine and full of unconditional love that we were all wiping our tears away upon the conclusion. The emotional night continued with a slideshow depicting our lengthy journey through the foster care system and our arrival home. My mom then proceeded to sing a song with her friends, Rainey and Laura. This was a song called "All I Really Want for Christmas is a Family." This song resonated in my heart because it was one that I listened to repeatedly in the car nearly every day prior to our adoption. The song shared a sad story of a young boy whose only wish was to have a family for Christmas. To hear my Mom sing the words to the song that had meant so much to me cannot be described.

For the final part of the ceremony, our family of four was called to gather around the small table holding the candle. As Pastor Dexter prayed for our family, we each lit one small candle. We then proceeded to join our four flames together to light the large, central candle that was adorned with our family photo. The lighting of this candle symbolized our unity as a family; we were four individuals who God had joined together as a single family unit. To watch that flame rise up gave me a sense of pride and empowerment. We were the Taylor family. This moment will forever be etched in my mind. Years later, this candle resides in our china cabinet. Once each year it is brought out to commemorate our adoption day. Each time we light that family unity candle, I am thankful for my forever family.

The celebration continued late into the evening as I danced with family and friends.

The laughter and tears of joy that filled the room were evidence of the happiness that flowed from our hearts. I had never felt this amount of love. For the first time in my life, I truly believed that I deserved to receive it.

As my parents thanked the guests for coming, Mom announced that God was calling her to move into the area of foster care and adoption. I had no idea at that moment that she was in the beginning stages of starting Mercy for America's Children which would later provide me with an avenue to give back to others. Our lives were about to change again.

–18–

Giving Back

As the next few months passed, we established a normal family routine. For the first time, I felt like I had a normal life. I was doing well in school, was playing sports, was developing friendships, and was experiencing more typical kid concerns. The thoughts of my past often flitted through my mind, but I was learning to face them courageously so I could then put them aside. I had finally begun to release the shame that I had carried for so long. In the place of guilt and shame, I began to develop a sense of pride that came from being chosen to be part of a family. This family had chosen me, fought for me, and were determined to help me achieve my goals and dreams. For the first time I had aspirations. Since I no longer carried overwhelming fear and worry and fear, I was able to focus on growth and change.

I often wandered into Mom's office and saw her looking at profiles of children awaiting homes on the Adopt U.S. Kids website. I knew that her heart was heavy as she thought about all of the children in the system who would not have a happy ending like ours. She began to study the statistics and learned further details about the process to foster and adopt in North Carolina. I had only been with this family for a little over two years, but during that time, I had learned so much about my Mom who spent countless hours in conversation with me. She had proven time and time again that she was a woman of selfless action. I knew her well enough to know that she was planning something big.

A family meeting was called. I had already anticipated this discussion. She was ready to act. Mom shared that she had felt a strong calling to resign from her 17-year career as a special education teacher to start a non-profit organization to promote and support adoption of children within the foster care system. She had not yet worked out the details financially or otherwise but was extremely passionate about her desire to answer this call. My dad was immediately supportive and simply decided that we needed to step out on faith and pursue this dream. We prayed for family guidance as we embarked on this new journey.

As I have stated, my mom is a woman of action. Once she had her mind set, she moved forward with intense drive. The organization was named Mercy for America's Children. Non-profit status was achieved. A mission statement was created. By-laws were established and a board of directors was selected to help guide the start of this organization. Mercy for America's Children officially began in March 2011. I stood back and watched this group of individuals begin to change lives for the better.

Although I was young, I had a strong desire to get involved in this organization that had been created by my family. I wanted to help others by sharing my past experiences. One year after its inception, I approached my mom and suggested that we create a Mercy for America's Children Kid's Division. When I was in foster care, I often felt very isolated and misunderstood. I wanted to offer kids in that same position a sense of hope; I wanted let them know that they were not alone and that someone did understand. The M.A.C. Kid's Division was officially founded in 2013 and included programs such as support groups, mentoring programs, specialized trainings, and special events for the children and families. The purpose of the M.A.C. Kid's Division was to promote a sense of belonging for the children who have spent time in foster care. By sharing the story of my past and mentoring children who were in the process of being adopted, I continued to find additional healing for my past wounds.

As I became officially involved in the organization, I began to feel more comfortable in sharing my story and began to speak in public venues to crowds of 200 or more listeners. I began speaking on a regular basis at churches, fundraising events, in promotional videos, and at charity galas. My story has also been featured on television and in multiple magazine and newspaper articles. Each time I am given an opportunity to appear publicly, I am truly thankful for the opportunity and give all the glory to God; this is His story and I am simply allowing Him to use it to reach others. This has never been about me but about how my story can help others. I am truly honored to have the opportunity to give back through leadership. While I am hopeful that I can make a difference in the lives of children, I am the one who receives the blessing each time I see a hopeful smile on the face of a child who has experienced pain similar to mine. Their smiles give purpose to my story. That is the true gift for me.

Mercy for America's Children has grown at a tremendous rate. I am awestruck as I watch the growth and expansion and witness the families that are now being served through support programs, including a behavioral support team, academic support team, specialized trainings, support groups for adults and children, a lending library, and 24 hour access to help and support.

I now serve on the Board of Directors for Mercy for America's Children as a Child Representative. As I sit at the table with these passionate leaders, I dream of the future. I am certain that we will continue to change lives at a staggering rate. I plan to be an advocate for change. I am devoting much of my time to studying psychology, working with children who have experienced sexual abuse, learning about trauma and attachment issues, and studying the foster care system. Over 400,000 children are in foster care in the

United States. Many of these children will have stories that end very differently from mine. The ability to use my past to create change provides me with a sense of empowerment. I look forward to seeing how God will continue to use my story in the future. I plan to remain open and willing to follow His will for my life.

–19–

Reflections

Since I have decided to devote my life to helping others who have experienced traumatic pasts similar to mine, I am often forced to reflect on my life. When I look at photos of myself as a young child, I often do not recognize myself. Those photos depict a child who was hurt by those around him, a child who endured a painful journey of abuse and neglect. I see so much fear in the eyes of that child. I am often saddened when I look at the pictures of my former self. As much as I would like to shred the photos that remind me of my journey, I know that each and every one of those painful moments have shaped me. Each ounce of suffering is part of my story.

Both children and adults often ask me how I was able to move beyond such pain at an early age. I have reflected on this with therapists and counselors over the years. The answer is quite simple. God brought me into a family that not only allowed me to feel and process every bit of my pain, but they experienced the pain alongside me. They took this journey with me; I was never alone. I am still amazed by the pain Mom and Dad experienced when hearing about my past. As I have learned to trust and truly love, I now understand how that works. I now love my family so deeply that when they are hurting, I hurt along with them. I now have a full understanding of what family truly means. When I was living in the abusive situation, I never imagined having the ability to love so deeply. While my mom and dad were always sympathetic to my past experiences, they continually pushed me to overcome fears and obstacles. With each victory, I became more confident in my abilities. Perhaps the most obvious factor that helped me overcome my past is simply stated as unconditional love. Mom and Dad made it clear from the moment I walked through the front door that I could do nothing to make them stop loving me. As most children in foster care do, I had to test this theory through misbehavior. Time and time again, they proved that they would remain by my side forever. They loved me even when I was unloveable. Over time, this destroyed my protective wall, and I was able to let them into my heart.

While I found healing for much of my pain, it was not an easy process. I was forced to face my demons directly in order to remove them from my life. I have now been with Mom and Dad for over six years, and I still deal with some residual effects that creep into my life from time to time. I have learned to cope effectively, but I still have a fear of heights, do not like to be startled, and prefer to be in close proximity to my family. My previous story provides clear reasons for these issues that come and go. However, they no longer have full power over my life because I have connected each one to my past experiences. Once I understand their origin, their power dwindles.

I also accept the reality that our family is different from most. I was not given the gift of a healthy family unit until the age of eight. Our family was forged through adoption. Like most teenage boys, I like playing football, enjoy spending time with my friends, and love playing the occasional video game. However, I am different in some ways. While most teenage boys want independence from their families, I enjoy every single minute I am able to spend with mine. The gift of time with my family was shortened by my time in foster care. I am fully aware that some day I will need my full independence, but for now I want to enjoy typical family activities, such as snuggling on the couch to watch a movie, playing monopoly on the back porch, or playing a family game of basketball. I continue to crave conversation and frequent interaction with this family that God has given me. I know that I am overly attached to my family, but I embrace that difference and feel no shame in that admission. My parents are not only my guides in this life, they are also my best friends. Because we traveled this painful road step-by-step together, we created a bond that can never be broken. I have a strong desire to remain close to my family throughout my life.

As I think about my future, I am filled with hope. I am certain that my past memories will rear their ugly heads on occasion, but they no longer have power over me. My parents have given me a clear example about following God as he leads; I plan to follow their example. When I envision my future, I have plans of becoming a psychologist. I hope to someday find the wife that God has chosen for me and become a father. My dream is to continue living very near Mom and Dad so that we can continue to live life together. I want to continue the work that I have been doing with Mercy for America's Children and will strive to fall asleep at night knowing that I have made a difference in this broken world.

I still have the dog tag with that amazing bible verse that I clung to so often in times of tragedy. It is well-worn from being gripped so tightly over the years. I have it safely tucked into a hope chest that was handcrafted by my grandfather. The words from Jeremiah 29:11 have become a reality instead of just a distant dream. I know that God has plans for me, plans for hope and a future. While God did not cause my pain, He has shown me how to use it for good. For that reason, I am thankful for my journey. Sharing the story of my journey from trauma to triumph is a true honor. While a few cracks remain, I am NO LONGER SHATTERED!

My Forever Family

Adoption Day
November 2, 2010

Having fun with Dad

Showering Mom with kisses

My brother and best friend

Speaking at the 2014 Charity Gala

Inspirational Quotes

There are several quotes and bible verses that served as inspiration for me throughout my healing journey. Listed below are some of my favorites.

Jeremiah 29:11

> "For I know the plans I have for   you" declares the Lord, "Plans to prosper you and not to harm you, plans to give you hope and a future."

Rumi: "You have seen my descent, now watch my rising"

Psalms 55:22

> Cast thy burden upon the Lord and he shall sustain thee: he shall never suffer the righteous to be moved.

Resources

Foster Care and Adoption

www.mac_cares.org : Mercy for America's Children is a non-profit organization devoted to promoting and supporting adoption of children in the U.S. Foster Care System. Please visit this website to get started in the process of adopting or fostering.

www.adoptuskids.org : Adopt U.S. Kids explains the process to adopt through the foster care system. They also have a photos of children who are awaiting adoption.

www.davethomasfoundation.org :
Dave Thomas Foundation. Visit this
website to learn statistics and facts
about adopting through the foster care
system.

Child Abuse / Sexual Abuse

www.stopiitnow.org: Provides
information to victims and parents,
relatives/friends of child sexual abuse.
The site also has resources for offender
treatment as well as information on
recognizing the signs of child sexual
abuse.
Hotline: 888-PREVENT .

www.d2l.org: Darkness to Light. They provide crisis intervention and referral services to children or people affected by sexual abuse of children. Hotline calls are automatically routed to a local center.
Helpline: 866-FOR-LIGHT
            (367-5444)

www.rainn.org: Rape, Abuse and Incest National Network provides valuable set of resources for victims of sexual abuse.

Sneak Peak

Here is a sneak peak from the next book to be released. "Behind Their Smiles" is a book written from the perspective of an adoptive parent who openly shares her emotions and experiences as she travels the journey of healing with her sons.

This was the moment. The moment that would forever change our existence. This was the moment that would determine whether or not I would be granted the gift of becoming mother to two boys who were nothing short of miraculous. Although I did not give birth to them, I knew in the depths of my soul from the moment we connected that they would become ours. I glanced down at the dog tag that was adorning my neck. It had become a symbol of bravery, a symbol of patience, a symbol of hope. The tag was inscribed with the verse, "I know the plans I have for you, plans for hope and a future" I stealthily tucked this token into my shirt as we prepared to hear the final verdict from the judge who had been entrusted with deciding the fate of two boys who had experienced a living hell during the most crucial years of life. After a total of seven days in court, everything came down to this defining moment. The room was painfully silent. Every single breath could be heard. As I gripped Mac's hand, I could literally feel his pained heart pounding in his chest. With each heartbeat and bated breath, we were waiting. We waited for the words to come from the mouth of the judge who had heard over a week's worth of testimony. Surrounded by our family and friends, this battle for normalcy and permanency would soon end for these two precious boys who had experienced horror beyond imagination at such an early age. The moment was here; the stern judge reached for his gavel and called the courtroom full of spectators to order. With one final lift of his hand, he gently tapped the gavel to the worn oak desk and stated the words we had been longing to hear, "The boys are hereby granted to Mac and Pam Taylor." Every ounce of my being was overwhelmed with relief. We had been given the gift of ensuring that these boys were never to be hurt again.